CW01649171

Visions of Greenwich Reach

by

Terry Scales

A revealing insight into twenty of the artist's major river paintings, with extracts from his Thames Diaries.

To Lynda Cecil.
with all best wishes.
Terry Scales.
June 6th 03.

First Published in the United Kingdom
in association with Aspen Creative Resources Limited

Blue Anchor Press, 12 Prior Street, Greenwich, London SE10 8SF
Telephone: 020 8853 3730
www.blueforce.demon.co.uk/terry scales

British Library in Publication Data.
ISBN 0 9535 4781 7

Terry Scales gratefully acknowledges the assistance of the London Borough of Greenwich (Time to Celebrate Awards) and the Woolwich Development Agency, without whose support this publication would not have been possible.

To David and Delia

"A man who paints puts his heart on the wall,

and in the painting is the man's life"

John Minton. 1951.

Contents and Colour Plates

with extracts from his Thames Diaries

Introduction

It is a strange thing that both painters and writers commonly refer in their work to a time not of the present but one associated to their very early years. In Constable's later landscapes there are no signs of the steam engines commonly in use in the farming methods of that time. Much of Charles Dickens' and the Bronte sisters' material alludes to a period some thirty years past. Turner is amongst the few to grasp the contemporary moment. When he completed his masterpiece, 'Rain, Steam and Speed', the locomotive had only been in existence for six years. For most of us, time is a necessary filter, enabling us to understand better the experiences we have lived through. The present is too undigested. By the time we have understood the focus of our study, the subject itself has moved on. A new set of circumstances confront us and we stand before them as a stranger.

Such is the predicament for those of us born into families for whom the Thames had provided a means of survival for countless generations. We will never come to terms with the silent stretches of water once awash with ships queuing up to enter the 'Pool of London'.

While it was all happening, I did draw a great deal, kept detailed diaries and made a number of personally important paintings, but it was only when I perceived the extent of the decline and the closure of the London Docks that I really saw it as a matter I could do something about as an artist. Here I had one big advantage over other painters of the Thames.

During the time I completed my Fine Art Diploma at Camberwell School of Art, and National Service in the R.A.F., a five year gap ensued before I was summoned back to Camberwell to teach drawing. Firstly, I entered a Fleet Street studio specialising in film posters, where I was constantly told, '..my figures were not pink enough...'! Needless to say, this did not last long. At a complete loss, I finally accepted the obvious and took a dockers brief in No.1 Sector, Surrey Docks. This allowed me to shape for work along the whole of the Bermondsey waterfront, from Tower Bridge to the Woolwich Ferry.

Since every male member of my family on both sides worked on the river, this was comparatively easy to arrange.

I am often asked, what influence did this first hand experience have on my paintings and wasn't I afraid it might damage my hands? To answer the first, when drawing a ship from afar, it must surely help to have some insight into how the massive vaults of the main holds are constructed, or to understand the juddering action of the steam derricks as opposed to the accuracy of the electric crane and what different types of tracery these might make against the sky.

I will let the great Victorian writer John Ruskin answer the second question for me. His practice was to encourage his students to busy themselves digging ditches and other menial tasks. The act of physical labour was spiritually purifying and much needed to balance the energy of the creative mind. He believed this passionately and so do I. Many artists today have become too separated from everyday aspects of life, taking refuge in technical cleverness, they dabble with snippets of video and shop-fitting exercises better suited to the context of 'Harrods' or 'Heals' superstores. Why is this when London is so rich in texture and visual imagery?

The answer might lie in the observations of the neo-Romantic artist John Minton, addressing a gathering of students half a century ago.

> "The painter today will only discover his personal idiom very late in life: the process of artistic digestion will be so lengthy. Finally one comes to the importance of subject. It is something to do with having a real love for it and an anxiety that it will escape him, and not just tolerating it as a possible subject. A man who paints puts his heart on the wall, and in the painting is the man's life."

This is as true today as it was in 1951.

There is indeed an anxiety to paint the last working wharves, Greenwich being the last stretch of London's river where one can look in both directions and still see ships discharging. They desperately need a guardian angel to protect them from the onslaught of development. Whatever the future holds, there is still much to be done. In this Millennium Year, we have seen the giant 'Catherine Wheel' on the South Bank and 'The Millennium Dome' on the peninsula dramatically change the skyline, and the proposed Cruise Liner Terminal also looks very promising. My colour plates end with a glimpse of things to come, the cruise liner, 'Cable-Innovator', occupying the mooring frequented by so many illustrious ships in the past. Shimmering white and high against a backcloth of the Isle of Dogs, it represents a vision of a glorious future and one that is utterly in keeping with our proud maritime traditions.

Deptford Creek, June 1949

After drawing all morning the interior of Queens House Greenwich for architecture studies, I made my way home via Deptford. Creek Road is long and uninspiring but at canal bridge I stopped to peer through a gap between some tall wood palings.

Two hundred yards away I saw a collier ship riding high in deep water beside a drab wharf. A westerly wind was blowing smoke from a powerhouse obscuring the little I could see through the thin mist. Apart from this, no movement of any kind disturbed the scene. It resembled a frozen tapestry, silent and very private.

A tram passed by rattling the ironwork of the bridge and causing me to pause in the sketch I had begun. The next day art school friends accused me of *"...doing an old master..."*, by deliberately losing the edges of my forms. So much for truth in front of nature!

Footnote
Decades later I discovered the sketch and made this painting from it.

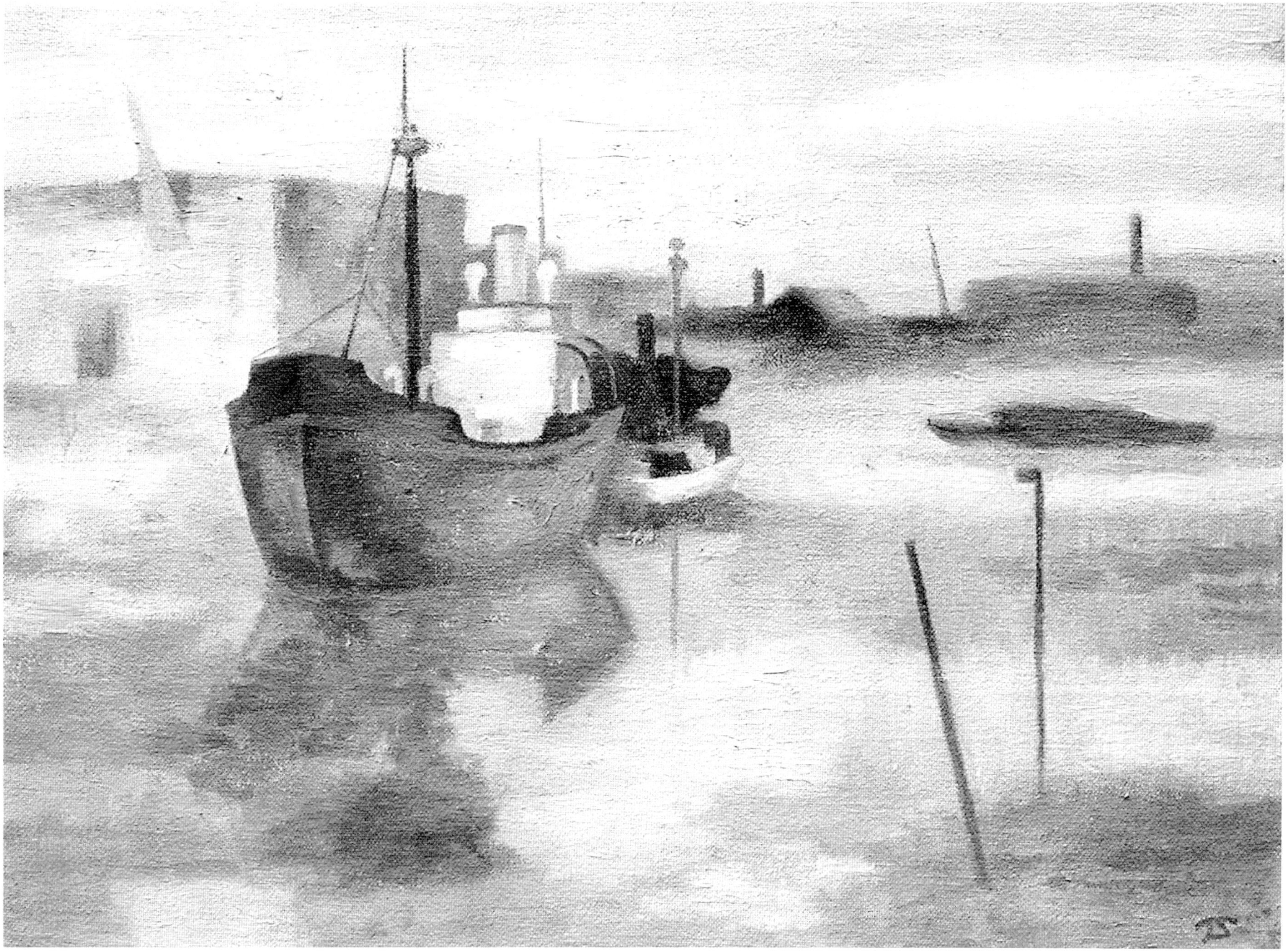

Morning Mist, Deptford Creek, Oil, 1949

Somewhere Along the Surrey Canal, 1955

My diary notes for 1954-55 record a number of drawings made along the Surrey Canal, mainly in sepia ink. Leaving Surrey Docks, it crossed under Evelyn Street Deptford, wandered on past the Old Kent Road Gasometer and then at Peckham split into two branches. One continued to the wood yard at the foot of Peckham High Street, the other moved west to terminate at Walworth. Along its route were a number of charming bridges, stables and wharves mainly trading in timber transported by barge from Surrey Docks.

What emerged from my studies was a composite picture with no one place in mind. My view of the humpback bridge was typical of those the canal traversed in the back streets of Deptford, Peckham, Camberwell and Walworth.

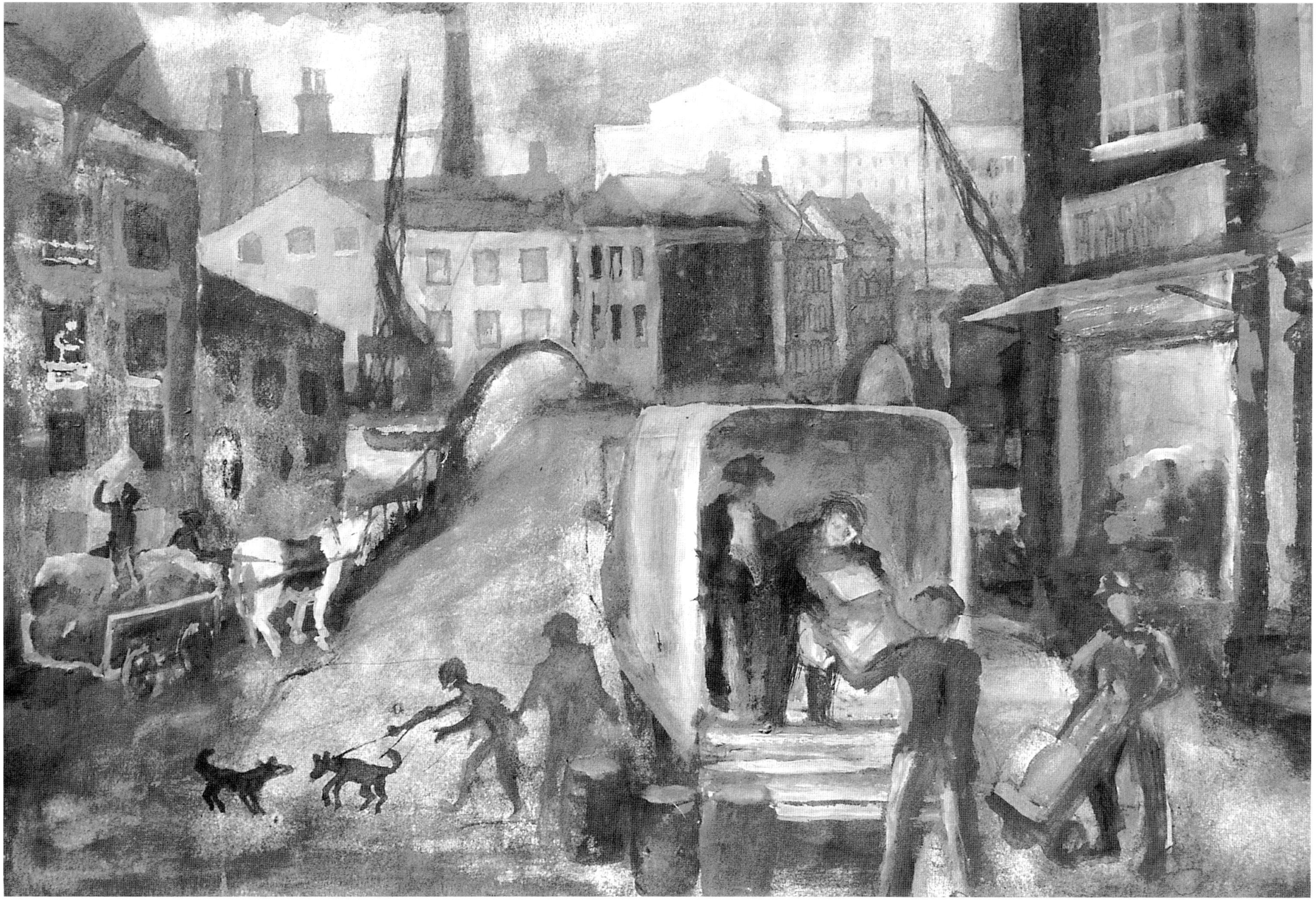

Somewhere Along the Surrey Canal, Ink and Gouache, 1955

Two for the Barge, 1957

On being demobbed from the R.A.F. in 1954 I faced something of a dilemma. All my Camberwell Art School friends had entered the teaching profession but, at twenty-one years of age, I felt too young for that. Since the 1880s, every male member of my family had worked on the river and it was decided I should do the same until such time as I might determine what to do. Thus from 1955 to 1960, I found myself working on hundreds of ships and barges of all shapes and sizes. As part of the huge workforce of No. 1 Sector Surrey Docks, I could be sent from the pool to any one of the numerous wharves from Tower Bridge to Woolwich and, more often than not, in Surrey Docks itself.

At these times I was too busy to draw but made numerous thumbnail sketches and, more importantly, stored in my mind a mass of images to be rediscovered later. The scene opposite, which could be anywhere along the southern shoreline illustrates the moment when the crane returns the empty sling to the waiting barge-hands. It is swiftly caught by one docker whilst the other makes ready to attach the next load. As the crane takes the weight, a lack of concentration now could result in the loss of a finger trapped between the bale and the tightening sling.

I witnessed one such accident in the hold of a ship in Surrey Docks. A spectacular scene followed where the injured man, ashen faced in a state of shock, was strapped tightly to a stretcher and whisked high out of the hold by the same crane that just minutes before had caused such a trauma.

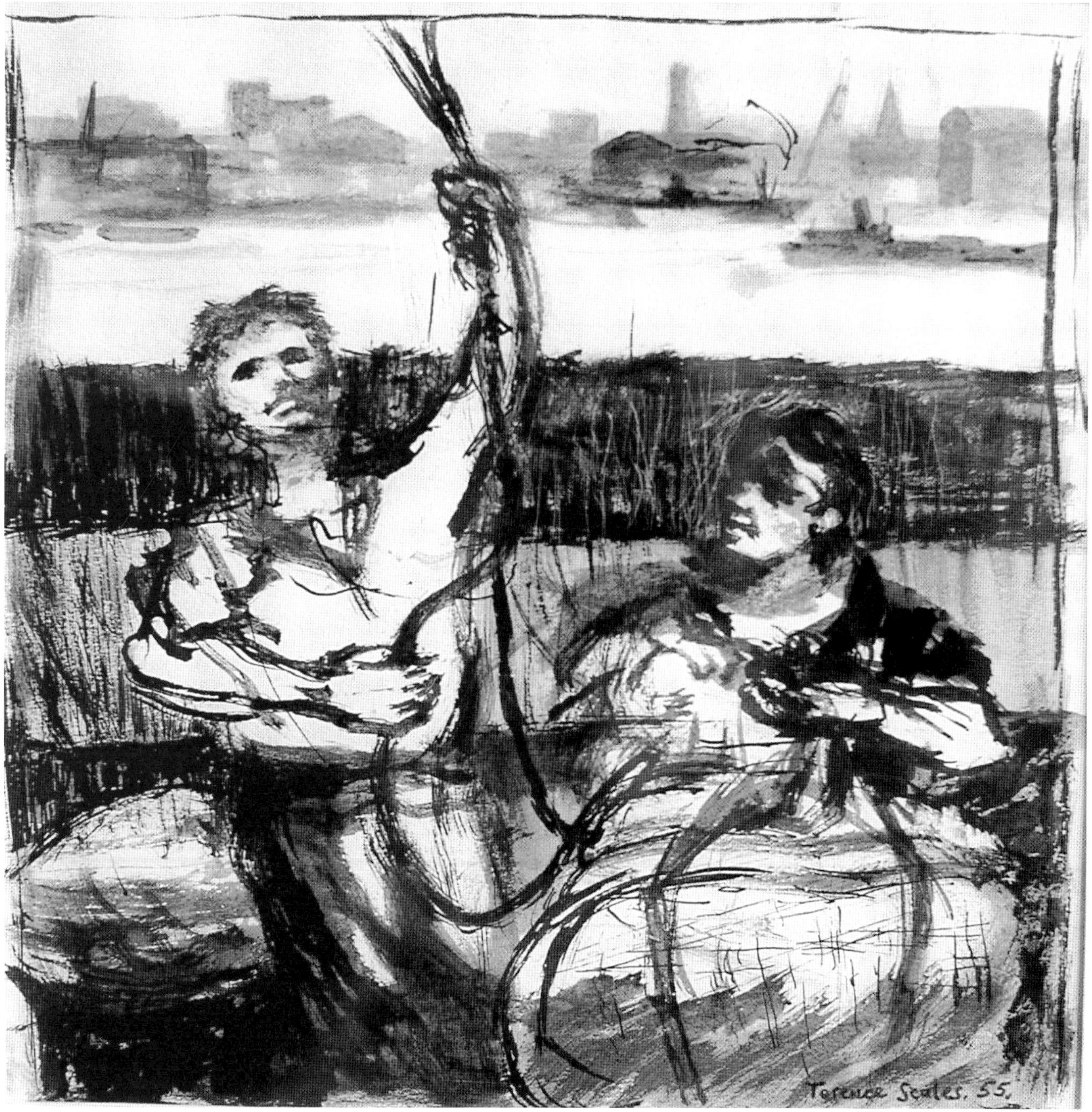

Two for the Barge, Indian Ink Wash Drawing, 1957

Timber Going Overside, Surrey Docks

My time in Surrey Docks coincided with the last big boom period of the Pool of London. My memories are one of a furious activity everywhere with barges swarming around each ship and the waters yellow from the flotsam of timber strips fallen overside. From June onwards ships from Norway, Finland, Russia, Sweden and Canada would queue up waiting for a berth. They would not wait for long. Crack stevedore gangs worked through the long hot summers discharging deckloads of striplings and deals into barges where each unit of timber was methodically placed in rows parallel to the length of the barge with cross-binding timbers placed every so often to stabilise the load. After reaching a certain height a bridge of heavy deals was constructed across the central width and sets continued to be lowered by a derrick onto this, preventing the weight of the new loads dislodging timber already stowed into the Thames.

Occasionally a ship would appear listing badly to one side, gently towed by a tug to its mooring. Caught in rough seas her deck cargo had shifted causing an uneven distribution of weight and she was lucky in the circumstances to make port safely. The stevedores task here was to unload from the side highest out of the water until she reached even keel. This they did with great expertise.

As a painter I could only look on at this wonderful world of action, enjoying the vast variety of hues within the spectrum of even one colour, from the darkest ochres to the palest of creams. The hiss of steam winches, hooting tugs and the crazy angles of ships' derricks plunging up and down made the term 'dynamic' an understatement.

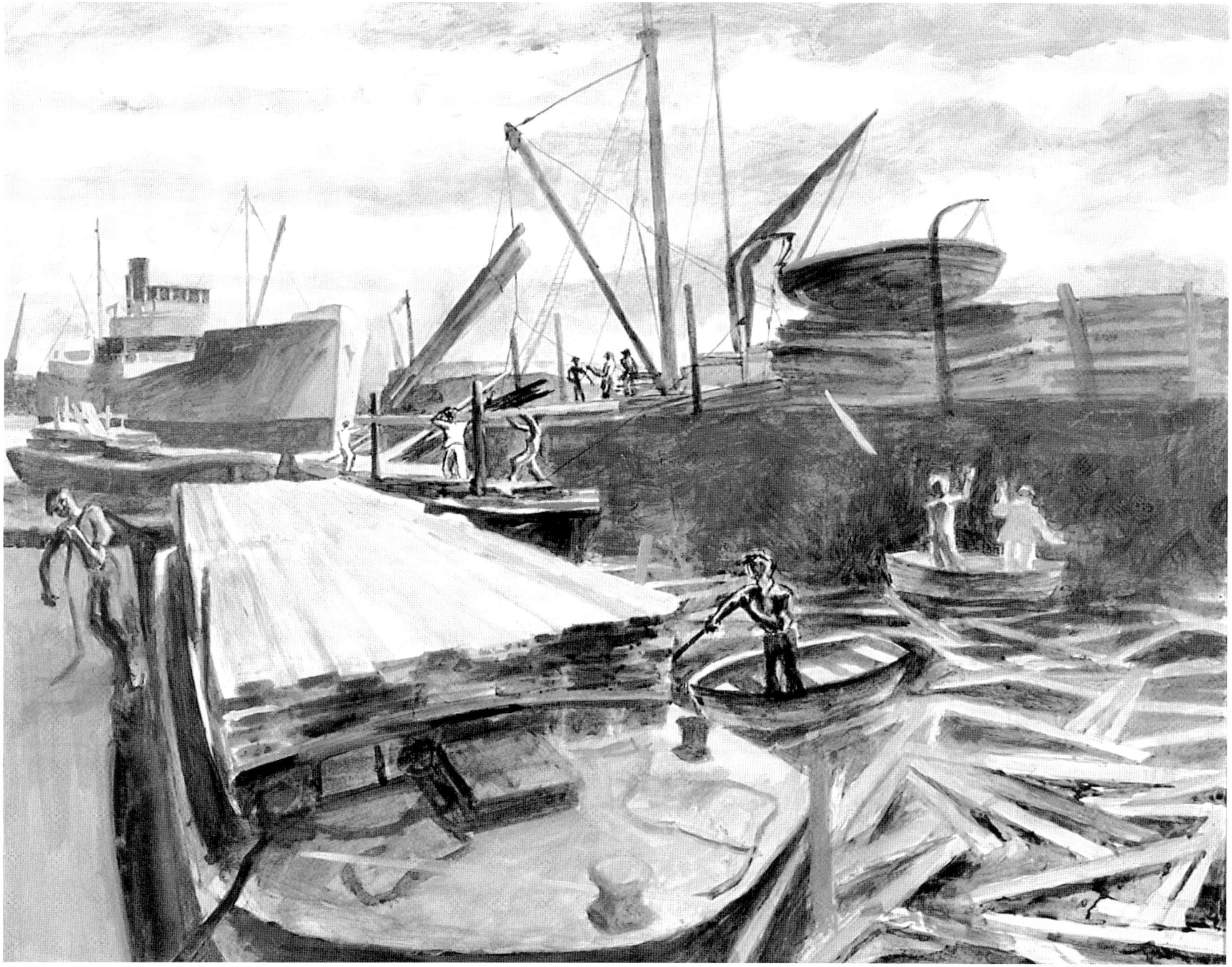

Timber Going Overside, Surrey Docks, Sepia and Gouache, 1958

Deal Porter

Half superman, half circus acrobat, deal porters were a group unto themselves, born into it, father and son, generation after generation. As a child I first saw them working in the wood yards by Cherry Garden Pier, fearlessly striding to the top of the stack like mediaeval soldiers storming the heights of a palisade.

A series of shallow sloping planks created a dangerous path to the summit. With a heavy deal on their shoulder and a measured rhythmic step they ascended, taking care to control the 'bounce' which each step created. Too much bounce and they could lose their balance but this rarely happened. After many years of this labour, deal porters often developed a permanent slope on the carrying shoulder.

Footnote
This wash drawing was composed from the odd sketches made in the 1950s but mainly inspired by memories from my childhood. Finally completing it in the early 1980s, it could be said to have been 'on the brew' for forty years, 1940-1980.

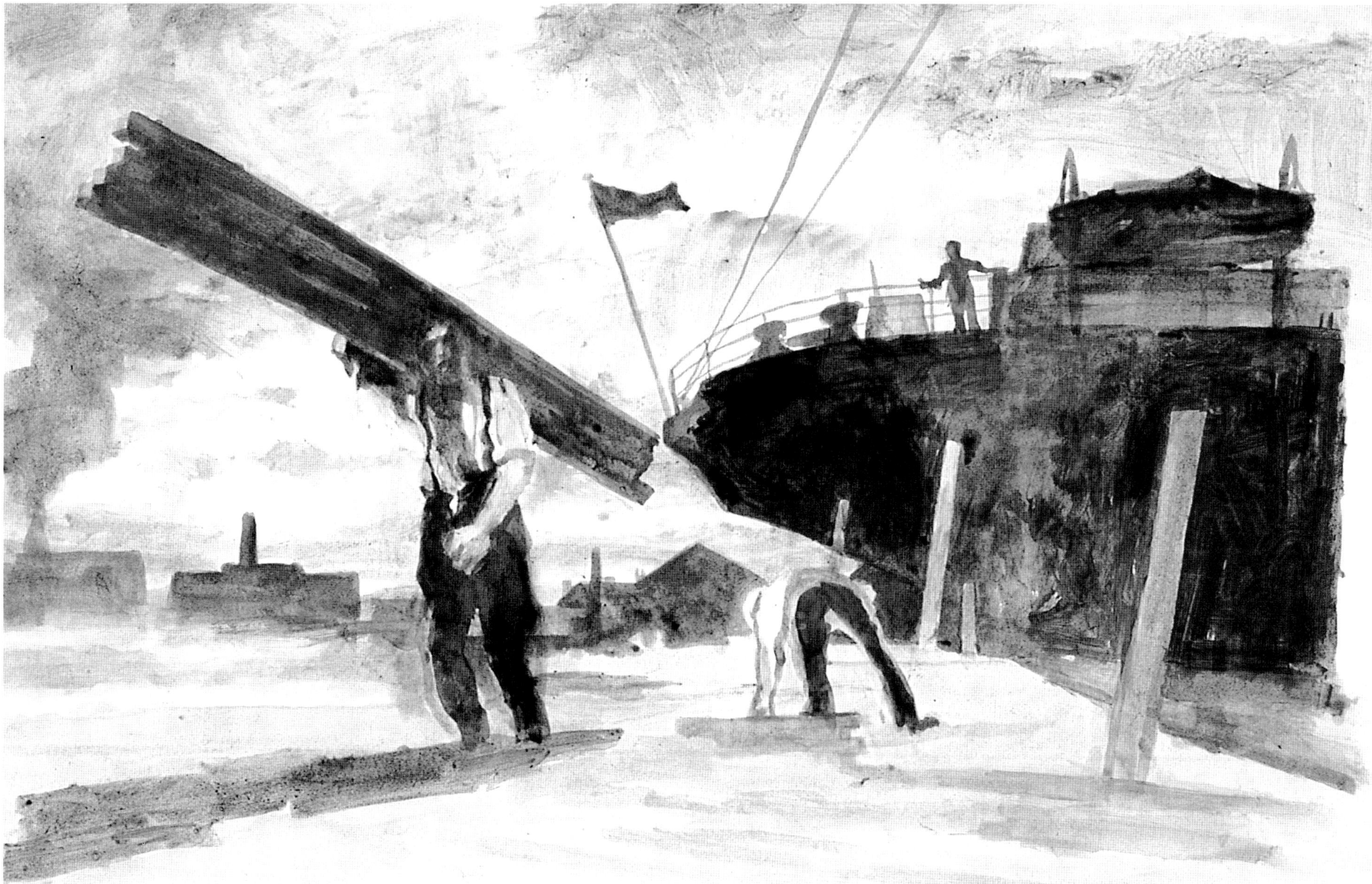

Deal Porter, Indian Ink Wash Drawing, 1957

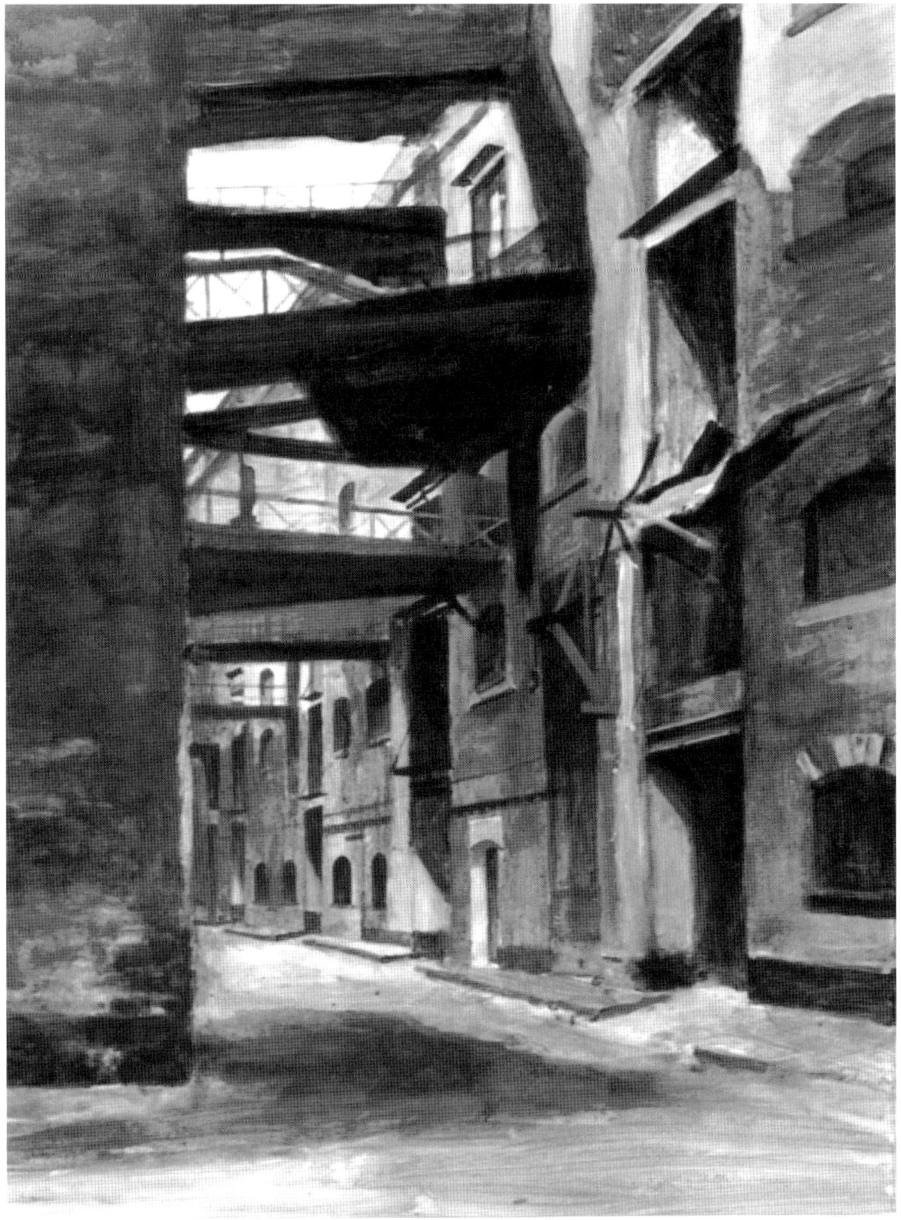
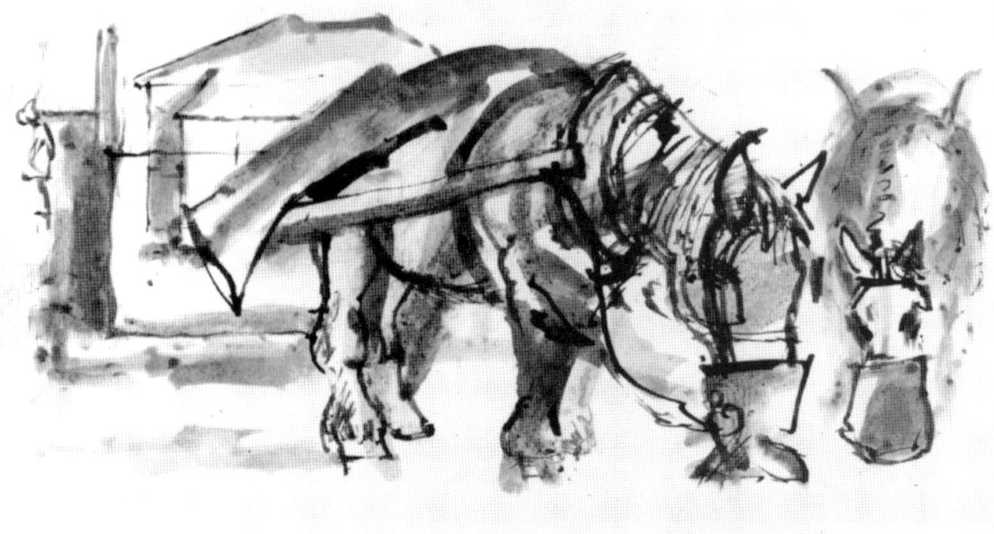
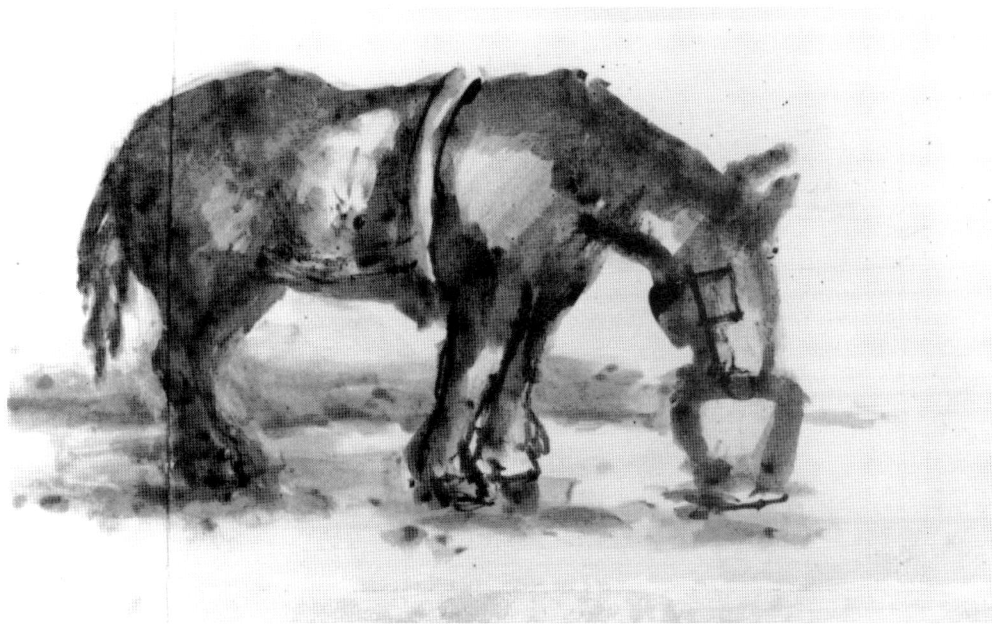

Butler's Wharf, Shad Thames, with two cart-horse studies, Sepia Wash, 1950-1980

Butler's Wharf, Shad Thames, Bermondsey

Slanting midday shadows and the sounds of contented munching. A symphony in sepia and old gold. Several cart-horses stand with bobbing nosebags. Tails flick spasmodically sending up clouds of flies to alight nearby. Soon they will return and the whole cycle will repeat itself until lunch is over and the tackle from the loop-holes above creek into action.

Two bags in the sling and down it goes. A brief pause, a yank on the pulley and the empty sling returns to be loaded again and again until the cart below has its sixty bags of flour and trundles off to the bakers.

As evening approaches the last cart moves away leaving only the aroma of spices and the flutter of pigeons.

Footnote
These sepia drawings are from a selection I made between the 1950s and the 1980s. There was such a Rembrandtesque richness to these scenes I am amazed so few artists took up the challenge. Perhaps, like me, they thought these subjects would be around forever. How wrong they all were.

The 'John Mackay', Transatlantic Cable-Layer, 10th June 1979

Down to Piper's Wharf where I saw a most elegant ship moored to the dolphins. The welders say it laid the transatlantic cable many years ago and belongs to Enderby's next door but is now retired.

Began work on a watercolour using gouache and some inks behind the protection of three barges. These diverted the wind somewhat but, by midday the first drops of rain fell, not a constant shower but just enough to sprinkle my paper and prevent further progress. Forced to take shelter in Piper's Wharf until 2 pm. Having established the rich rust red tones of the barges I changed to my finest sable brush to paint the delicate white superstructure, masts and funnel.

As luck would have it, a black cloud of smoke rose from the Isle of Dogs creating the perfect background silhouette for the ship's bridge and the strange drum on the prow from which the cable was released.

This scene epitomizes all that is exhilarating in Thames subject matter. Emblematic notes of primary colour singing out against a background of turbulent sky, light one minute, leaden dark the next with high winds pushing continents of cloud banks at ever increasing speeds. In the face of adverse conditions I feel today I captured something of this.

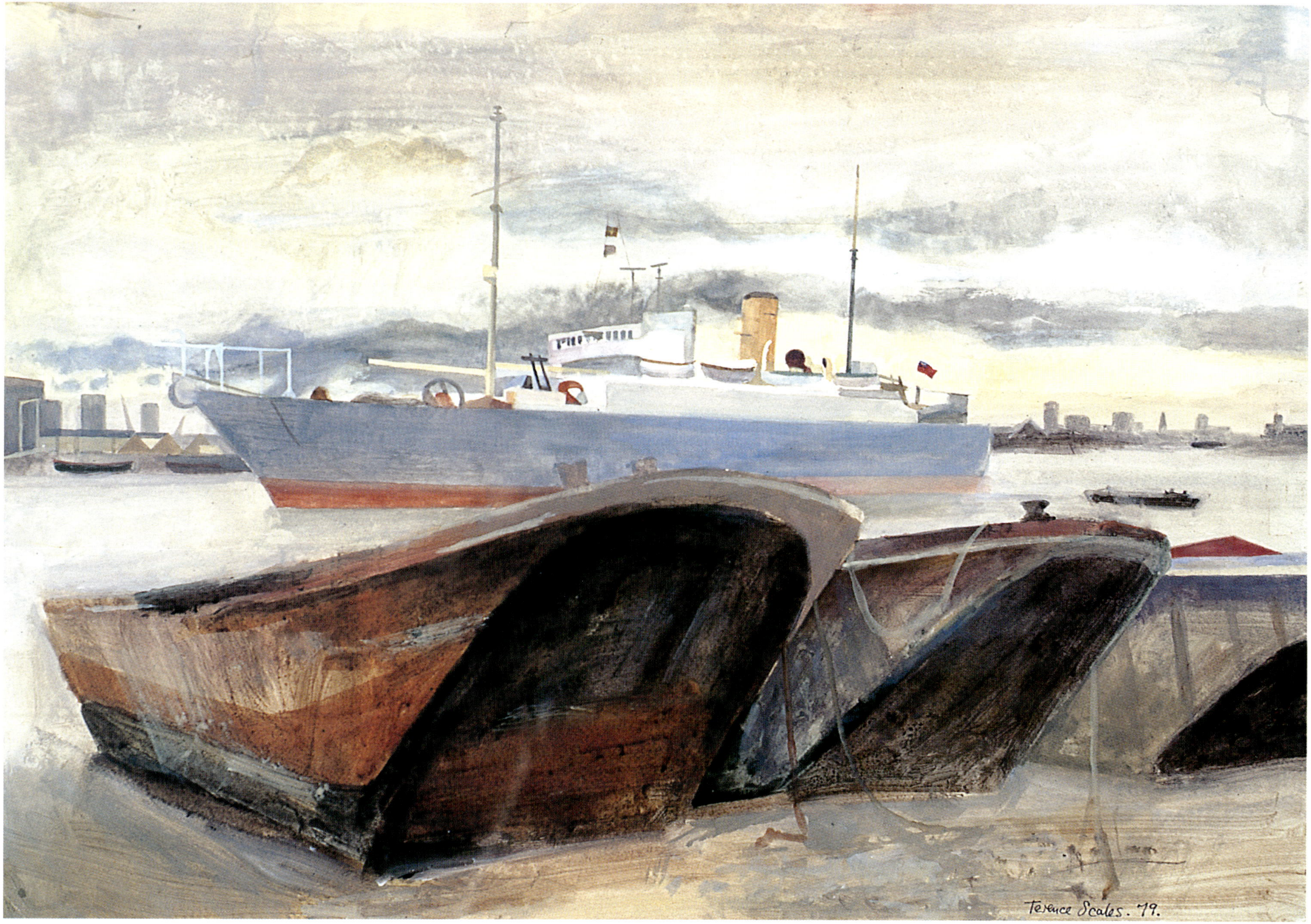

The 'John Mackay', Transatlantic Cable-Layer, Enderby's Wharf, Oil, 1979

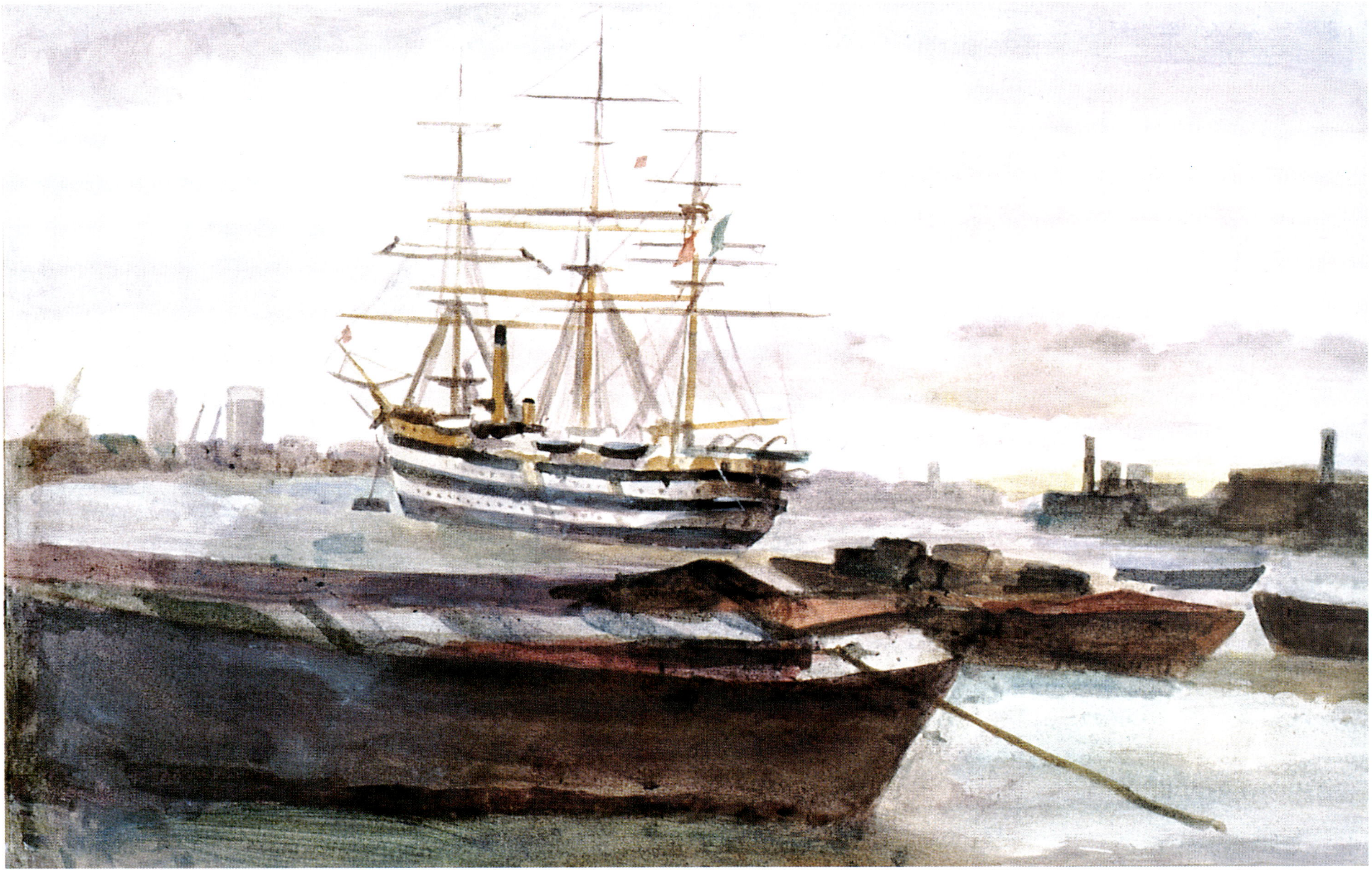

The Amerigo Vespucci, at Greenwich Reach, Watercolour and Gouache, 1983

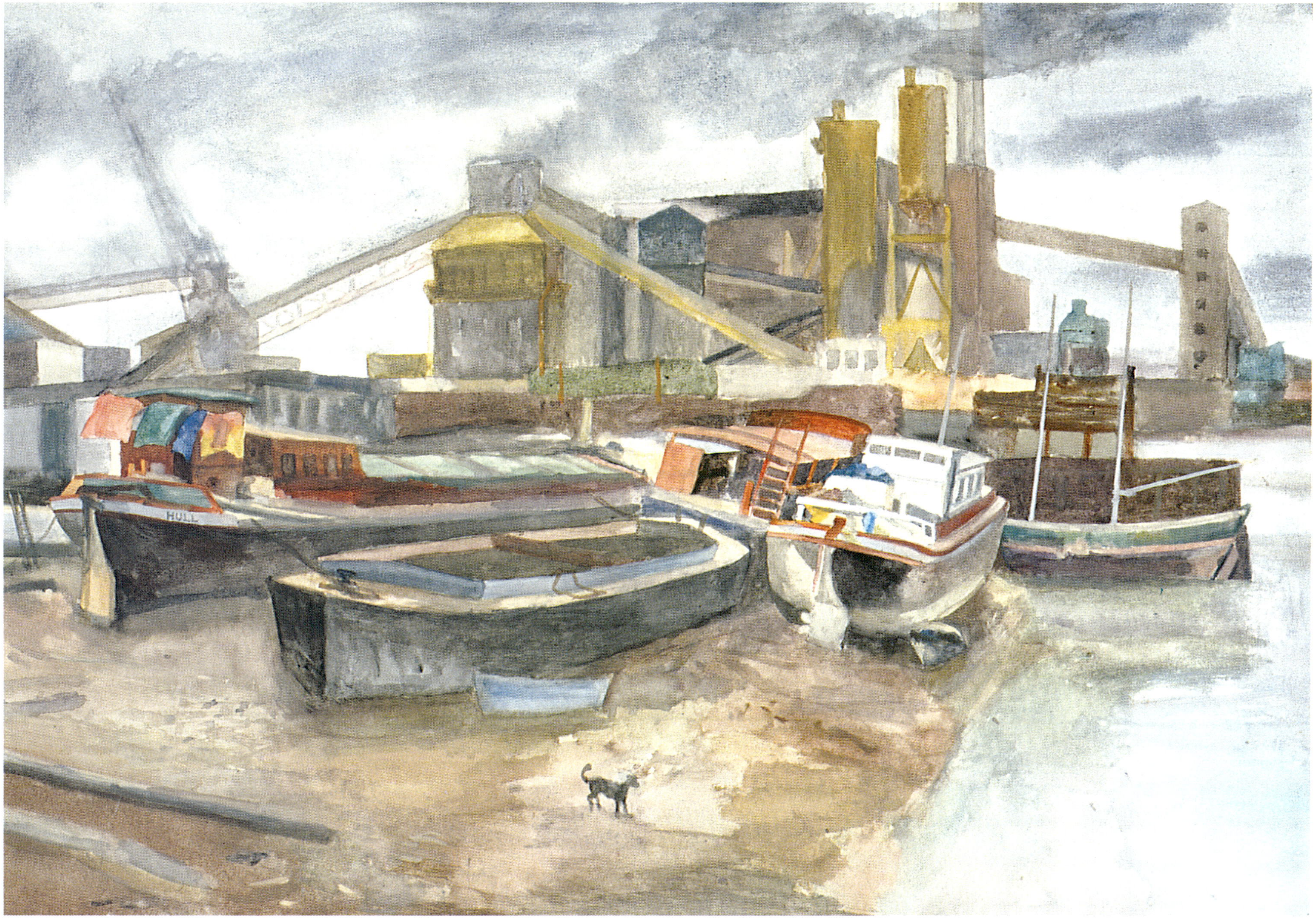

Mike Canty's Boat Yard, Watercolour and Gouache, 1988

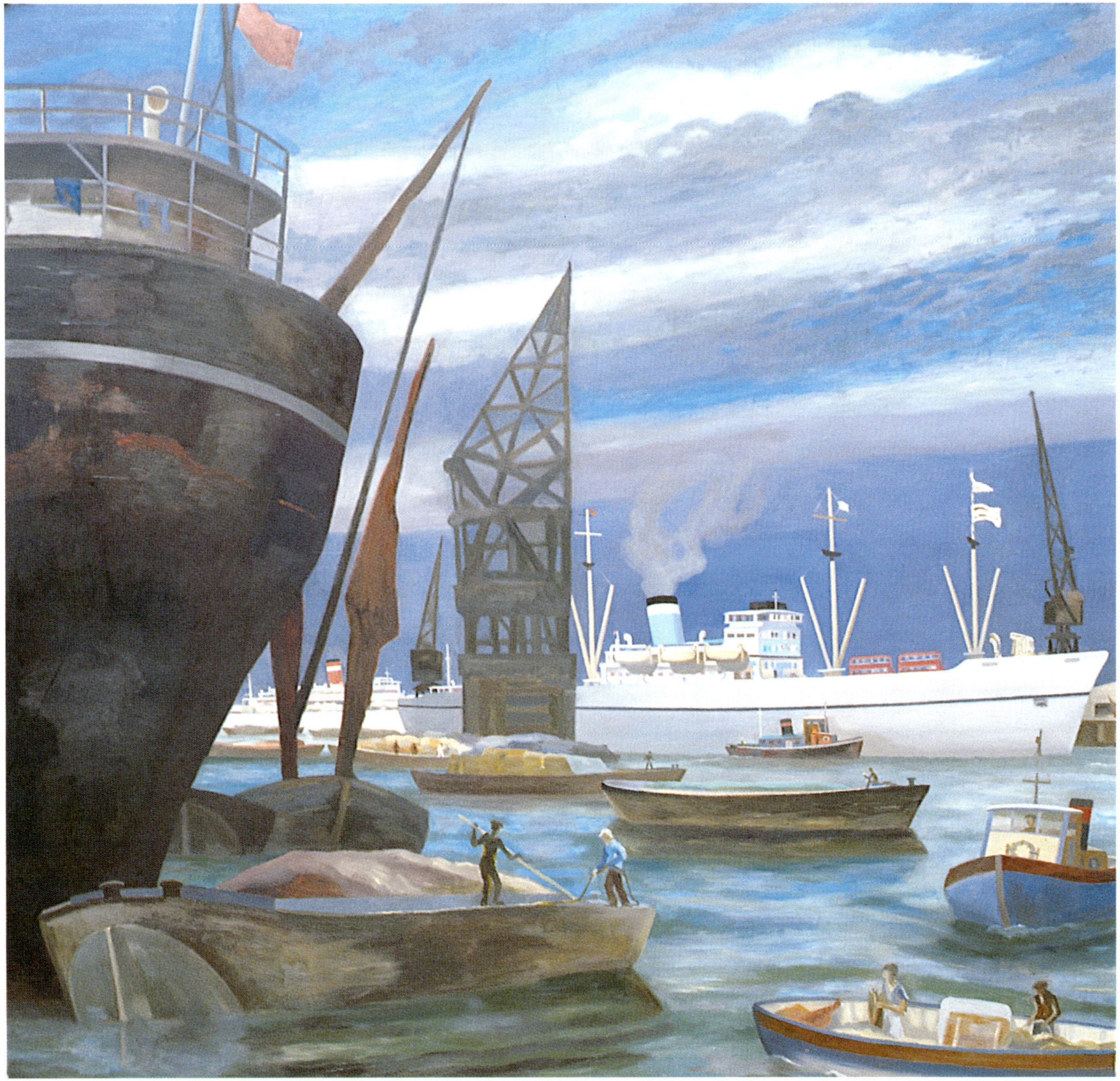

King George V Dock, Oil, 1980-1988

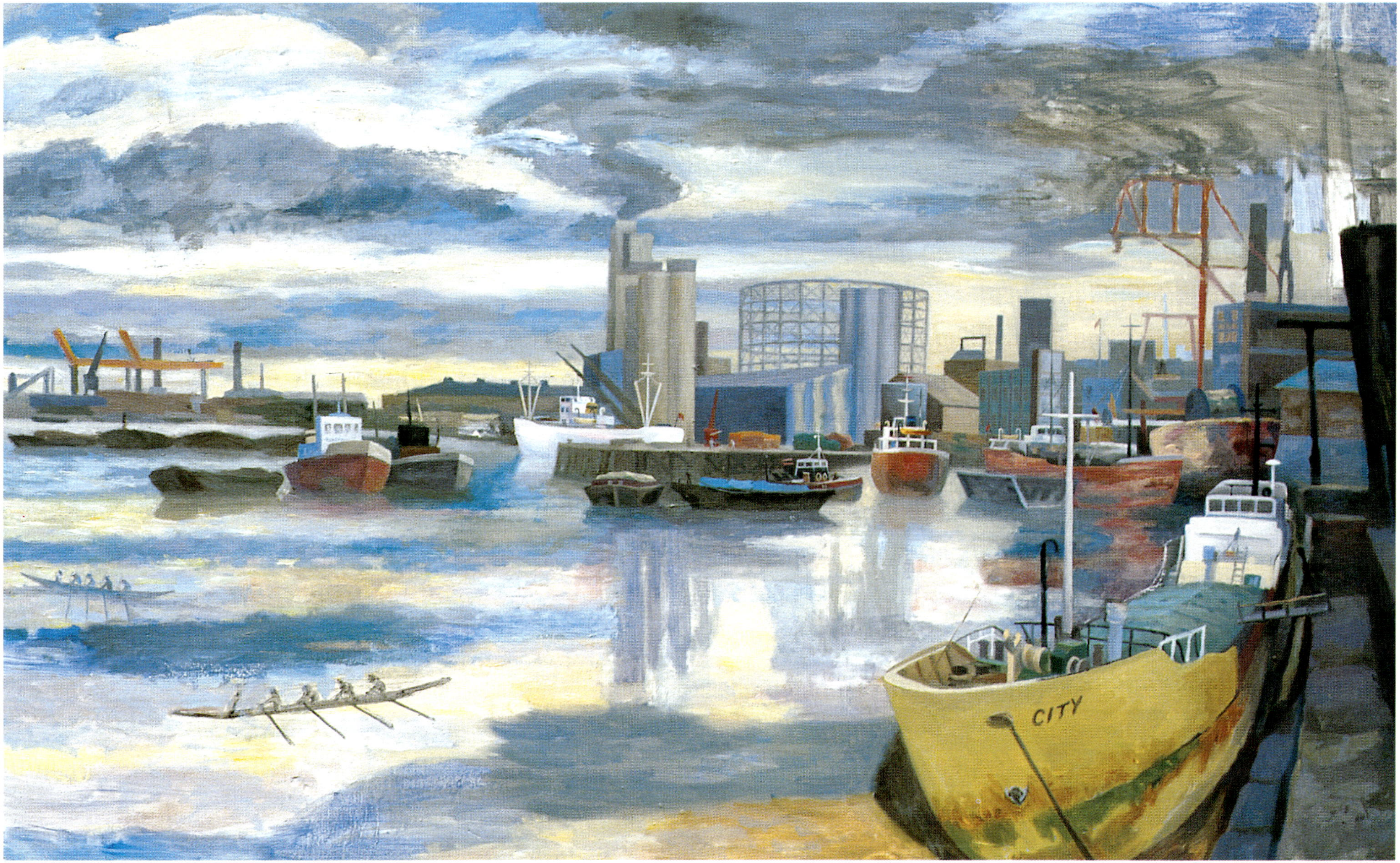

Greenwich Peninsula, Oil, 1986-1989

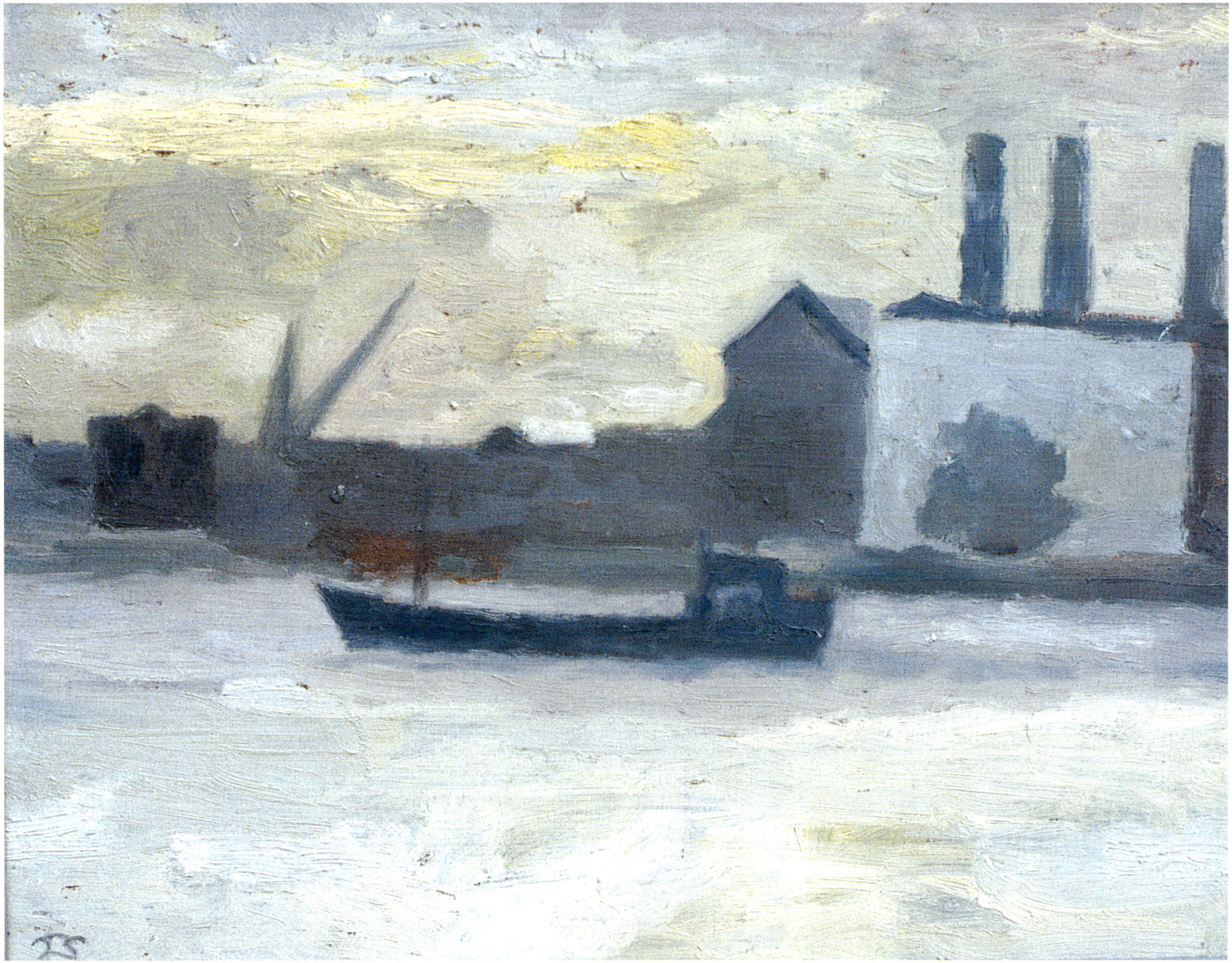

Black Ship in a Fog, Oil, 1990

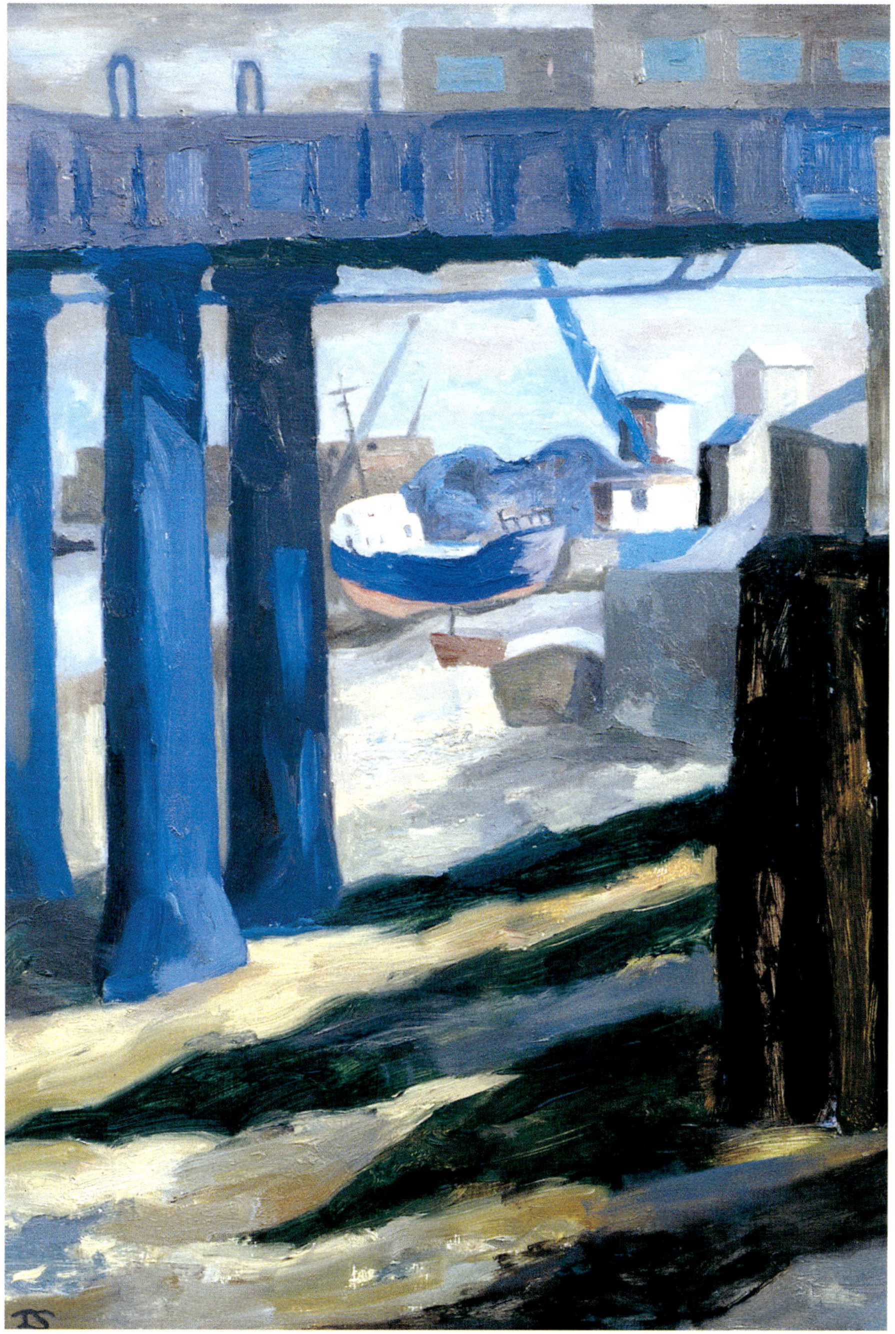

Under The Coaling Pier, East Greenwich, Oil, 1990

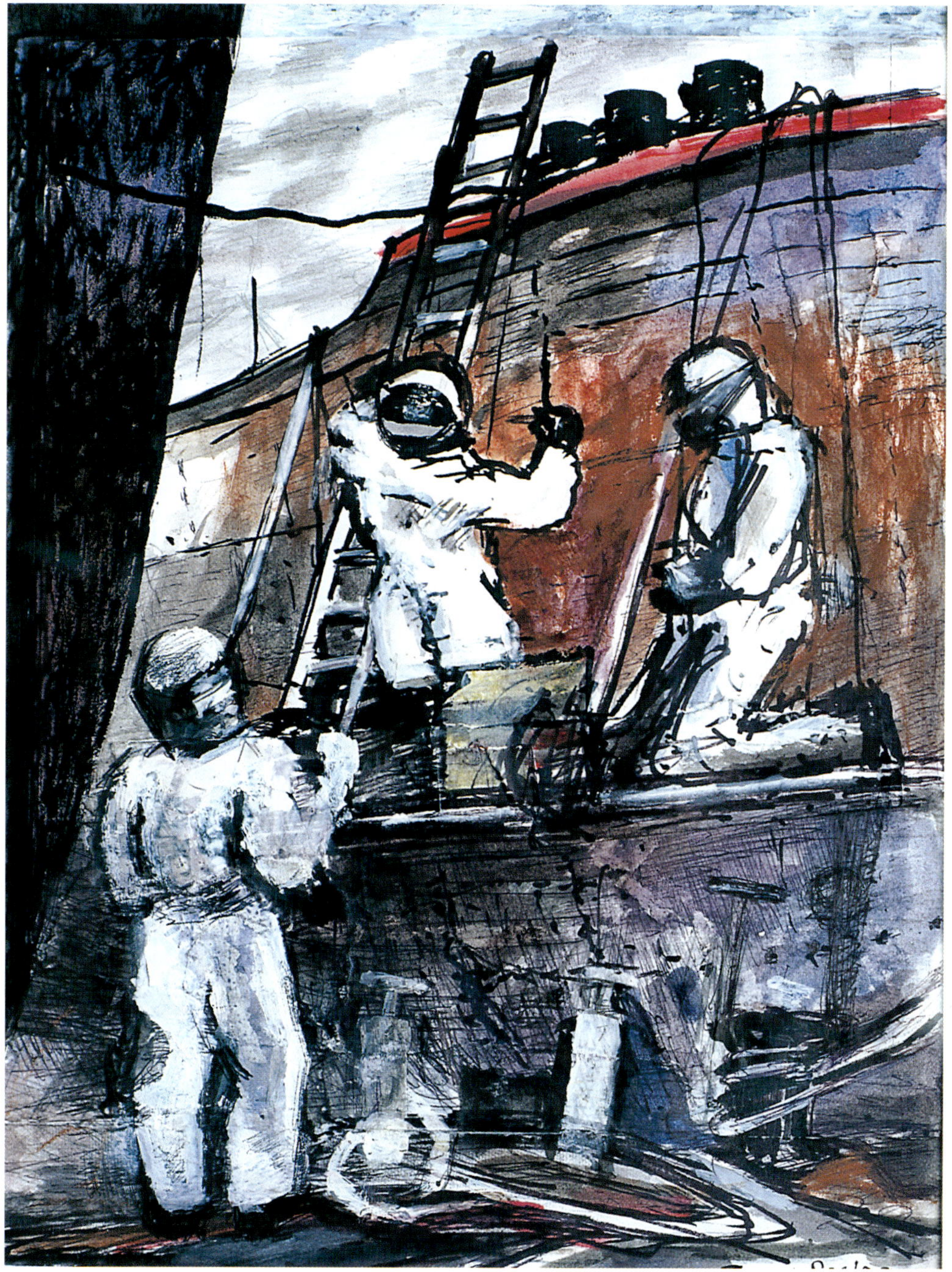

Welders at Piper's Wharf, Ink and Gouache, 1993

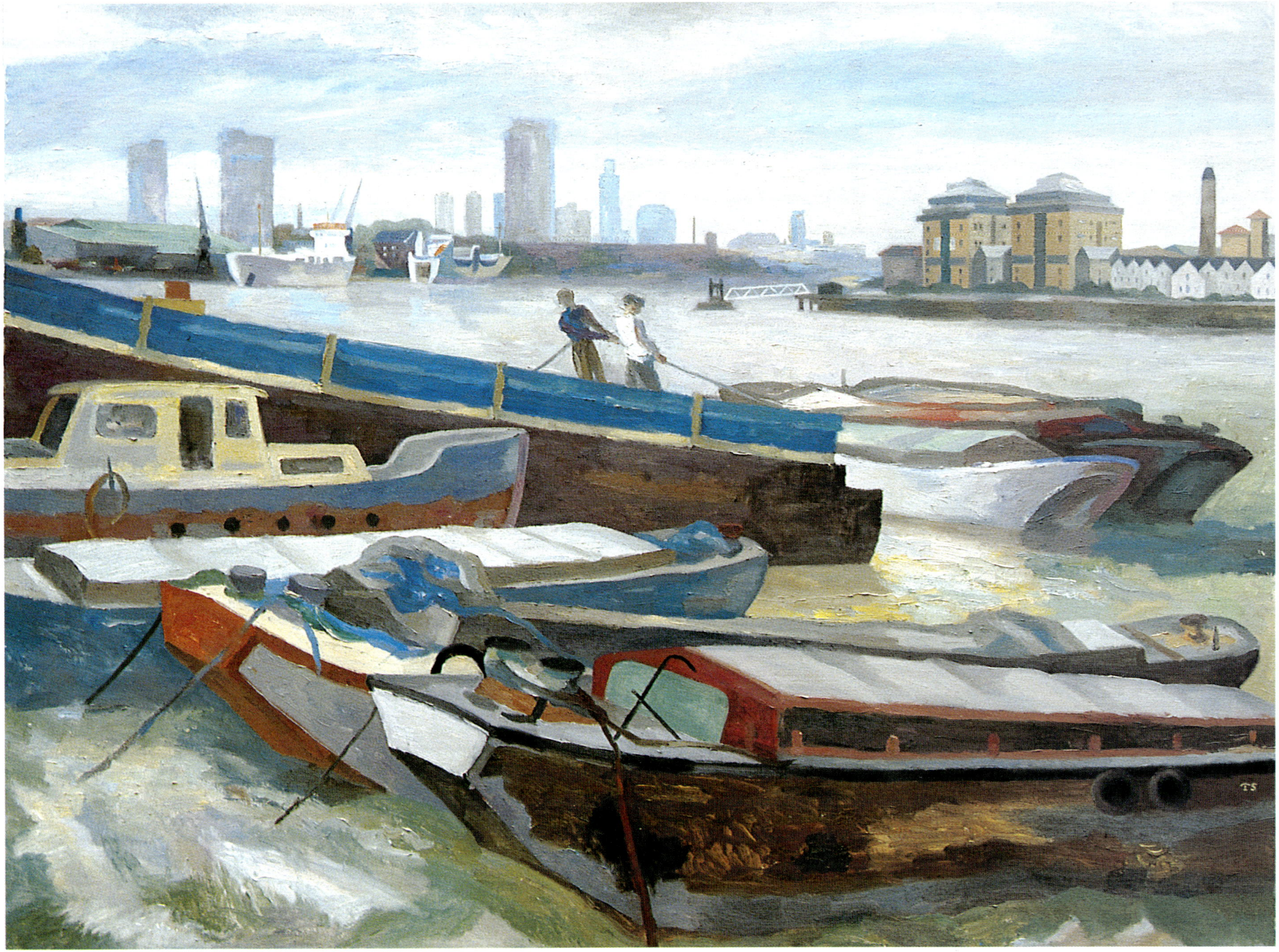

Pope and Bond, Barge Repairs, Oil, 1992

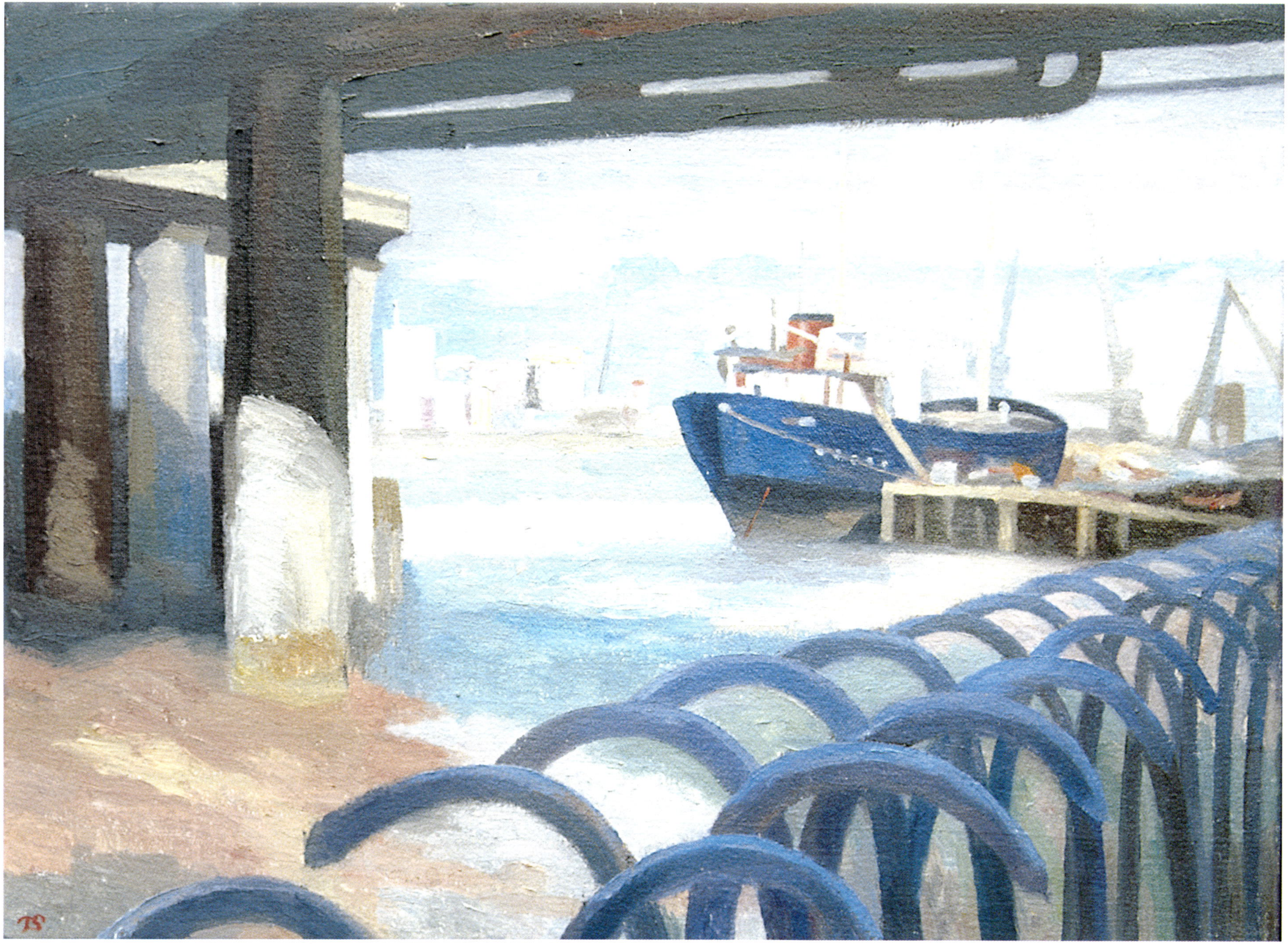

Last Ship from Anchor Iron Wharf, Oil, 1990

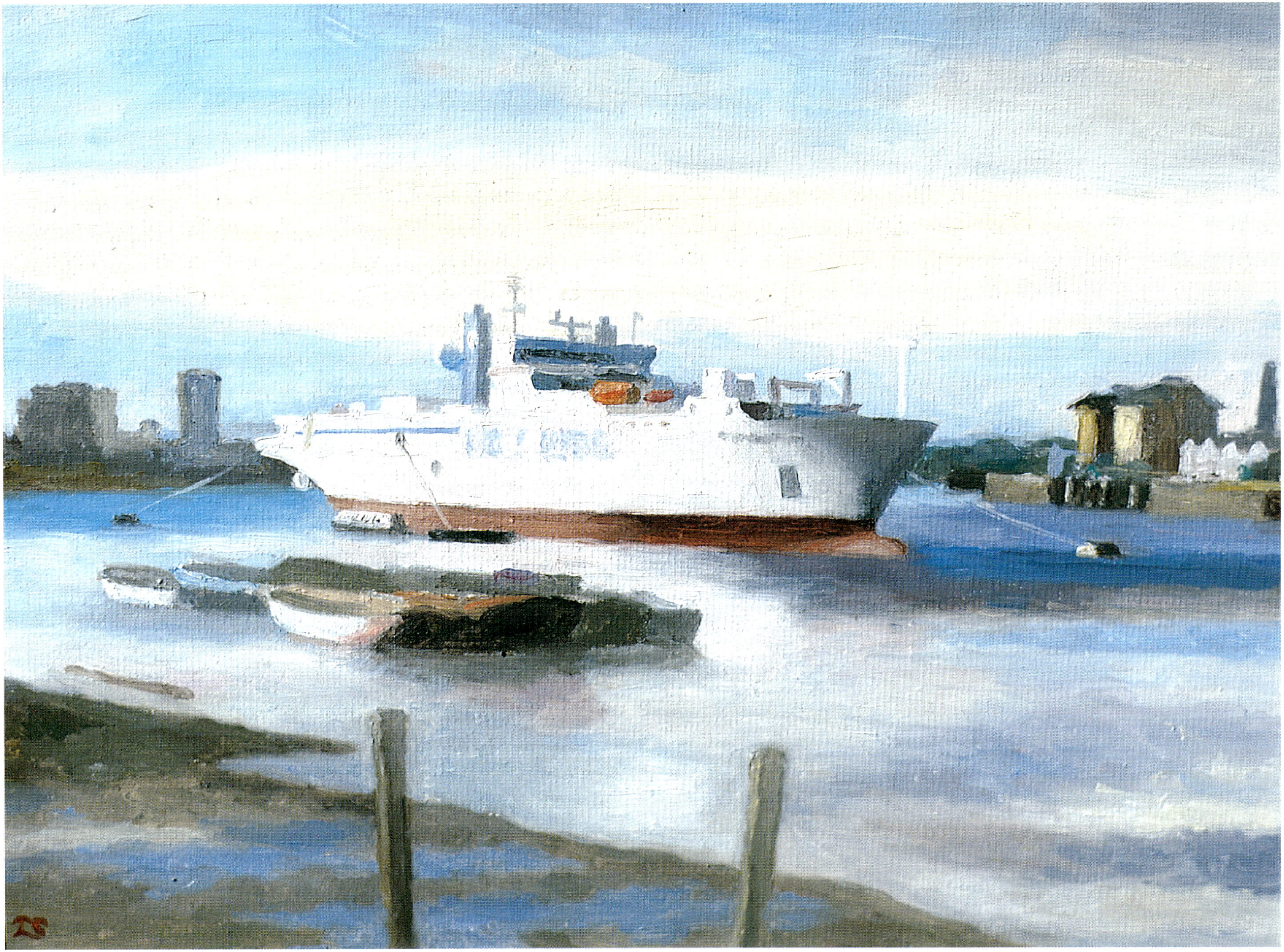

The 'Cable-Innovator', on a Courtesy Visit, Oil, 1996

The Amerigo Vespucci, 9th August 1983

Great delight today to discover the Amerigo Vespucci at anchor off Greenwich Pier. In spite of the large number of tourists, I worked flat out for three hours to produce this watercolour. Riding high, with bands of black and white from stem to stern, this much loved training vessel for Officers of the Italian navy is everything a sailing ship should be, the very epitome of national pride. We in Greenwich are lucky enough to have the deep water to accommodate such a beauty but, what should we make of the Thames barges nearby?

I have long held the view that the Thames Tug with its row of barges truly represents the spirit of London. Tough, reliable workhorses, there are some who see them as scruffy relics of a past age, preferring to see the banks of the Thames cleared of its indigenous industries and replaced by lines of expensive hotels. These people, I need hardly say, are not true Londoners.

Mike Canty's Boat Yard, 12th July 1988

Between the 'Gipsy Moth' yacht on the promenade and the mouth of Deptford Creek, lies a squarish inlet used as a boat yard. To reach it one has to go through a wharf on Thames Street and standing on the quay, look down over the jumble of houseboats, old tugs, steam launches and other craft undergoing repairs.

The tide was out when I arrived, leaving every vessel on a deep bank of mud, with the exception of one three-master with its stern afloat. A washing line hung by the poop deck of a motor barge flapping linen sheets of orange and green to liven up the puritan greys of the cement wharf behind. I so enjoy discovering 'hot colours' in a subject that I am inclined to overdo it but, here, the context was just right. The colourless sky and tidal waters together with the heavy earth colours of the power house, combined to make the perfect foil for the vibrant notes of the washing line.

It is often the 'incidentals' that make a painting. The viewer responds to the 'familiar' in an unfamiliar setting and the artist is often in urgent need to bring a visual shock into a work. A frequent incidental and one I am always grateful to find, is the 'lone dog'. Often a mongrel, it will suddenly appear from nowhere, as it did in this instance, to make a focal point, very precise and dead centre of the foreground.

King George V Dock, 1980-1988

A pale ship lies still under a dark sky, steam rising thinly from its black, blue and white funnel. Just below a row of Naples yellow lifeboats leads to the bridge all glistening white and delicately compartmented. The only sign that this is not a ghost ship is the surprise notes of cadmium red made by two double decker buses, part of the deck cargo. All other elements, the mammoth floating crane, the lightermen in the foreground, are just secondary actors on the stage.

I must now admit to using strong artist's licence. Normally I stick to the existing company colours as they appear on funnels and pennants, indeed, I embrace with open arms the chance to use such heraldic touches. In this instance, the Ellerman Liner, as I'm sure it was, disported just the wrong note of buff yellow at the base of its funnel.
This would have wrecked entirely the surreal-like mood I was trying to create, so by changing it to blue, I re-enforced this as the dominant value taking the scene out of the present and into a state of suspended dream-like time.

My motives in doing this were rather complex. I had visited King George V Dock less than a dozen times in my years on the river with only the slightest of sketches to show for it but my father had worked there most of his life. In the evenings I would hear graphic accounts of the ships he had worked on that day so I became very familiar with the great shipping lines from an early age. The Japanese 'Maru' boats, 'The Durban Castle', 'Empress of Montreal', here was all the romance of the high seas and my father was very proud to be a small part of this.

Surrey Docks was not without its own big ships and I remember with affection 'The Asia', a great Cunarder and especially the 'Baltika' from the USSR. To see it leave port at night was a wonderful sight. With martial music played at full blast and all lights ablaze, it said 'Goodbye' in great style. I see them - and paint them - as mythical giants, since they belong to an age when beauty on the ocean highways was in great abundance. Sadly, it is not the case today.

Greenwich Peninsula, 1986-1989

This particular oil painting was triggered off by my excitement at finding 'The City' at Lovell's Wharf one day. Yellow ships are not that common!

During the progress of an ambitious studio work many ships may come and go as the artist builds his collection of on-the-spot drawings. Having drawn a cargo vessel on Monday, its place will inevitably be taken at the end of the week by one of an entirely different shape or size. Both vessels present fine images and the dilemma is posed, what to keep and what to lose?

Sometimes the best solution is a visual overlapping where the hull of one ship accommodates the bridge and derricks of another. A late arrival on the scene can also create a stir. Such as was the case when a shimmering white ship took the place usually occupied by the little green coasters mooring at Tunnel Refineries, now known as AMYLUM UK.

With these challenges, an artist is more akin to the conductor of a symphony, pulling, pushing and stirring the threads together into a cohesive whole, rather than a reporter merely recording the facts.

Lost at Sea, October 1988

The switchboard at Lovell's Wharf is manned by a friendly secretary. My inquiries as to the arrival of shipping are always received in a spirit of helpful courtesy.

To my deep dismay I learned today that one of my subjects, the cargo boat, 'Lizzie', was in collision with another ship off the coast of Holland. It happened in thick fog and the damage was so serious she sank soon after. She was one of two vessels both painted cream and deep blue and named 'Lizzie' and 'Annie' respectively, probably after members of the company's family.

Deptford Creek, 7th February 1989

At Greenwich Pier I watched a large ship making up river on the tide. Steering over to the north bank it swept around in a quarter circle turn, headed back towards the south side and entered Deptford Creek.

I ran as fast as I could to Creek Bridge, just in time to see it edge alongside the quay by the cement wharf. Simultaneously and much closer to me, the motor barge 'Bert Prior' swung its stern around in order to pass under the bridge in reverse. Its birth at Prior's Wharf is just beyond but at this point the canal is too narrow for a craft of this length to turn again.

In spite of these skilled acts of navigation and the surrounding dust and detritus of the cement works, the canal presents a scene of classical serenity

Welders at Piper's Wharf, 20th June 1993

Something about the ponderous movements of these craftsmen reminded me of the great 'Crucifixion' etching by Rembrandt. Maybe it was the angle of the ladder, or the archaic ship's cradle, reminiscent of a primitive altarpiece. The cumbersome ritualistic way all three set about their tasks seemed like a tableaux from another time.

Piper's Wharf never fails to surprise me. It is by far my favourite spot along the river, with its unusual and unexpected craft awaiting repair. Some years ago I collected enough driftwood from its shore to build an entire garden shed.

Black Ship in a Fog, 7th March 1990

Returning from Aldgate via the Docklands light railway, I stood for a while taking in the unfamiliar view of the Greenwich shoreline at the furthermost bank of the Isle of Dogs. A slight fog hung over the water creating a curtain of dull silver and sulphur yellow space. The massive chimneys of Deptford Power Station looked even grander deprived of any detail. The fog allowing only the main silhouette and the surrounding leaden skyline to register.

As I looked on, a small ship passed silently by heading downstream. Black as a funeral hearse, it moved with the same gravity. At that instant it struck me forcibly that this was a metaphor for the sad decline of the river industry and I jotted down the basic lines on an old envelope, unprepared as I was.

On another level, this ship reminded me of Turner's great masterpiece, 'Burial at Sea', a memorial to his friend Sir David Wilkie who died on board the Orient on his way back from the Middle-East. Anxious to preserve the elegiac mood of my subject I began to work on a small oil panel and, after three intense hours, added the last touches of colour.
In spite of its modest size it has remained my most popular painting and is now in a private collection.

Under The Coaling Pier, East Greenwich, 6th May 1990

The old coaling pier was built to convey coal from collier ships to the great electric power station which so spectacularly dominates the riverside skyline at this point. Here we see the dynamic forms of industrial architecture at its most creative. Doric columns rise from the Thames to support a covered gallery that bridges a pedestrian path and continues on into the bowels of the powerhouse. Some decades ago water splashed down from the conveyor to the accompaniment of a monotonous clanking. It was the perfect site for the late Poet-Laureate C.D. Lewis to use as the setting in his murder mystery when writing under the pseudonym of Nicholas Blake. Now the conveyor is silent and the water cascade ceased long ago.

Taking advantage of the low tide I spot a ship lying on a generous strip of muddy foreshore. What excited me particularly about this scene is the resonant deep shadows created by the columns contrasting with the delicate creams, blues and white of the crane and ship's bridge. The effect of this is to make a pool of vibrant light in the centre of the painting in which the vessel becomes the central element. As much as I would have liked, I could not paint on-the-spot since the tide would soon turn. As I finished my drawing the water was inches away from my feet. Rushing back to my studio I began work at a very fast pace in order to capture the freshness of my experience.

Pope & Bond, Barge Repairs, 18th June 1992

"Excuse me for interrupting, but can you tell me what those ships are over there?" He pointed upstream towards the big roll-on-roll-off boats at Convoy's Wharf, Deptford. I paused in my watercolour to study the elderly couple before me. Both were soberly dressed and though obviously visitors, their accent gave nothing away.
"That is Convoy's Wharf," I answered, "and the ships come from Canada and Finland carrying reels of paper for the national press."
"It's so wonderful to see it all again. We left England in 1938, sailed from over there on the 'Dominion Monarch' to South Africa." He waved his arm in the direction of Canary Wharf and what was left of the old Millwall Docks. "Since then we've never been back." It was a deeply touching moment for them both and leaving them to their memories, I bid them farewell.

I pondered this interlude for some moments. It is a fact, we just don't appreciate the emotive power of the Thames and its related crafts and industries. We take for granted the eccentric shapes of the cranes, the algae fringed piles and the strange sounds of rusting fences flapping in the wind. It would be marvellous to see the shoreline busy as it once was but there is no denying, the unused lay-bys awash with the bones of abandoned craft, create their own romantic mood, a world of solitude and personal reflection.

I returned to my watercolour, the subject of which was 'Pope & Bond Barge Repairs'. This study was to aid me in a large oil painting of the whole curving sweep of the river around the Isle of Dogs. On a slanting jetty, two men hauled a white barge to shore. Between them and me lay an array of brightly coloured craft. The chunky presence of these pushed the space way back to a lonely looking pier over on the extreme point of the north bank. Also important to the illusion of distance were the tower blocks, sentinel-like ghosts from another planet, built behind the former Royal Navy victualling yards at Deptford. Their cold remote hue was exactly right for the tension between the hot busy foreground and the receding elements of the skyline.

In completing the work some six weeks later, I was pleased that the two figures played a vital role in defining the middle ground between the forward and furthermost space.

Footnote
In mid-July 1996, Pope & Bond found itself in extreme financial difficulties owing to the loss of a vital contract with Westminster Council. Failing lack of support and further contracts, trading ceased shortly after this date.

Last Ship from Anchor Iron Wharf, July 1990

Without any plan in mind I wandered by the Royal Naval college and saw the reassuring sight of three adolescent school girls, navy blue skirts tucked about their waists, wading out until the water reached their knees. With mock screams of terror they splashed each other and the sight of such a simple act of pleasure made my heart soar. In an age of hi-tech wizardry, nature contrives to have the last laugh.

I inwardly applauded their utter contempt for the hidden dangers of broken glass, pollution and all the other hazards real or imagined, that conspire to prevent a greater enjoyment of the Thames. In my boyhood we swam off Tower pier when the river was at its most polluted state but I never knew of any case where a child fell ill because of this. Since suicide attempts were far more common from the ramparts of Tower Bridge, a police launch stood by on permanent duty, saving many unhappy souls.

Seeing the figures in the water reminds me of a long-term plan to make a large 'Bathers' painting - a Thames equivalent to Seurat's great work in the National Gallery. I jotted down a few notes and continued on to Ballast Quay. Framed by the massive cast-iron columns of the coaling pier, lay a little gem of a ship, broad red funnel surmounting a white deck and blue hull, like a diamond set in an angular steel mount. In the foreground a row of curved palings echoed the blue of the ship's hull and created a complete composition. I drew for two hours to complete a detailed drawing.

Footnote
The following week, this berth ceased trading and by coincidence I had recorded the last ship to sail from Anchor Iron Wharf.

The Victoria Deep-Water Commission, 5th February 1990

The first day without rain and hurricane winds for two weeks. I decided to visit the Deep-Water Terminal on the Greenwich Peninsula to refresh my memory and study the tones in more detail. It is hard to pick up the threads of a working drawing I made two months ago but, once I arrived, the light was entrancing, dazzling bright in the centre of the river, fading off at the margins to a pinkish-grey.

I had some difficulty in identifying the original spot I had first drawn at as the cranes seemed to have been moved. These gigantic portainers are so high, they create an illusion of change at every visit. To relate their vastness to the minute details of the distant shoreline takes some optical adjusting but, this time, I experienced something I had never encountered before.

It is my habit to use the back seat of my Austin Maxi as a studio in uncertain weather - the space is quite generous. However, the dark interior had an electrifying influence on the already bright sheet of water. The ensuing dazzle caused an after-image effect, whereby vivid greens and yellows leapt off my white paper, destroying any attempt to focus on either the landscape or my painting. After five minutes my eyes became adjusted and using plenty of water, I managed to capture the relationship between the sky and the light on the river. I decided to go for the spirit of the place and leave all the details for another day. It had been a useful watercolour session and I reluctantly joined the queues of juggernauts pouring out of Blackwall Tunnel.

It is not just for money one accepts a commission, although that is very welcome. There is also the invigorating value of getting outside of yourself for a bit, away from well-trodden habits. With the Victoria Deep-Water Terminal I have been fortunate enough to be engaged to paint a scene I would want to paint anyway. The constraints however, are the degree of accuracy and detail applying to forms like the Stothard and Pitt crane and the giant portaine gantry replete with original lettering. These are shapes I might otherwise have simplified or changed in some way.

The client has the right to ask for strong authenticity and artists, from time immemorial, have had to strike a balance between these demands and the general spirit of the subject. The ensuing tension has added something special to many masterpieces.

Bert and James at Deptford Creek, 9th September 1990

Some paintings are doomed to go terribly wrong right from the start. However hard one tries, they seem to be fated. Equally, thank goodness, some paintings seem guided by a friendly spirit and almost paint themselves with the artist in a state of sustained joy. Such was the case with Bert and James. Named after members of the Prior family who trade at the wharf of the same name, they continue a long and honourable tradition of celebrating the birth of a son or daughter in good maritime fashion.

It is rare to see both vessels together in the creek and I spent the whole day drawing every detail, soaking up the cadmium reds confidently emphasising the bulwarks. On the quay behind, piles of bleached sand created a pleasantly organic depth, arrested by an assortment of ancient warehouses. The sky in such a busy scene was crowded almost out of existence but the tiny strip remaining was vital for the painting to breathe.

The 'Cable-Innovator', on a Courtesy Visit, 20th September 1996

The world's first purpose built, stern-working, cable-laying vessel at anchor by Greenwich Pier and despite the huge crowds of tourists on the promenade I managed to catch a few details. It is interesting to compare it with its predecessor on page 23, 'The John Mackay', then moored downstream at Submarine Cables, Enderby's Wharf. Here we can compare two state-of-the-art ships, one built in the 1930s and the 'Cable Innovator' launched in 1995, a pioneering addition to Global Marine System's present fleet. Although divided by some sixty years of changing design and innovation both vessels present a proud silhouette against South London's busy skyline.

It is good to know that some of today's ships are as paintable as the ships of the past and I eagerly await the opportunity to paint the anticipated liners visiting the proposed Cruise-Line Terminal. That will indeed be a feast.